HAPPY BIRTHDAY

TO

....

WITH LOVE FROM

....

And John

HAPPY BIRTHDAY—LOVE...

Complete Series

Jane Austen

Joan Crawford

Bette Davis

Liam Gallagher

Audrey Hepburn

John Lennon

Bob Marley

Marilyn Monroe

Michelle Obama

Jackie Kennedy Onassis

Elvis Presley

Keith Richards

Frank Sinatra

Elizabeth Taylor

Oscar Wilde

HAPPY BIRTHDAY
Love, John

ON YOUR SPECIAL DAY

ENJOY THE WIT AND WISDOM OF

JOHN LENNON

ROCK'S GREATEST DREAMER

Edited by Jade Riley

CELEBRATION BOOKS

THIS IS A CELEBRATION BOOK

Published by Celebration Books 2023

Celebration Books is an imprint of Dean Street Press

Text & Design Copyright © 2023 Celebration Books

All Rights Reserved. No part of this publication may be reproduced, stored in or transmitted in any form or by any means without the written permission of the copyright owner and the publisher of this book.

Cover by DSP

ISBN 978 1 915393 62 3

www.deanstreetpress.co.uk

HAPPY BIRTHDAY—LOVE, JOHN

The man who needs no introduction—John Lennon was born in Liverpool, England on October 9, 1940 to a teenage mother and a soon-to-be absent father. This unstable life gave him the foundations for rebellion and creativity as well as a greater freedom to become himself. When his Aunt Mimi presented him with a Gallotone guitar, John dreamed the dream of being bigger than his beloved Elvis. His Beatles' bandmate and co-writer Paul McCartney described John as the kid that all the other parents warned their children to avoid. But John Lennon was a true

Renaissance man; he went on to art college, acted in plays, drew cartoons and illustrated his own short stories and poems leading to the books *In His Own Write* and *A Spaniard in the Works*. Sample: "Jumble Jim, who shall remain nameless, was slowly asking his way through the underpants . . ." It is easy to forget that our working class hero, the artist who told us to Give Peace a Chance, had a very silly side to him. He even loved to play Monopoly!

With the unprecedented success and sensation that was the Beatles, John used his fame to promote real change. "Happenings" in the 1960's were the staging of artistic and political events, often grabbing the attention of the press. At his 1969 wedding to Yoko Ono, the pair staged their infamous "Bed-In" honeymoon for peace; protesting the Vietnam war for one week in Amsterdam and one week in Montreal. Moreover, this union gave the more mature John his second chance at fatherhood. It is wonderful that the last years of his life were given over to raising his son Sean and doing simple things like baking bread. Although he died tragically and far too young, John Lennon's life is a real example of what it means to live well. In truth, love is all you need. That, and the gift of his music.

John Lennon

When I was five years old, my mother always told me that happiness was the key to life. When I went to school, they asked me what I wanted to be when I grew up. I wrote down 'happy'. They told me I didn't understand the assignment, and I told them they didn't understand life.

"Part of me suspects that I'm a loser, and the other part of me thinks I'm God Almighty.

Music is everybody's possession. It's only publishers who think that people own it.

"Everything is clearer when you're in love."

I'm cynical about society, politics, newspapers, government. But I'm not cynical about life, love, goodness, death. That's why I really don't want to be labeled a cynic.

"Reality leaves a lot to the imagination."

I believe in God, but not as one thing, not as an old man in the sky. I believe that what people call God is something in all of us. I believe that what Jesus and Mohammed and Buddha and all the rest said was right. It's just that the translations have gone wrong.

"

Trying to please everybody is impossible—if you did that, you'd end up in the middle with nobody liking you. You've just got to make the decision about what you think is your best, and do it.

"

Well, pain is the pain we go through all the time. You're born in pain. Pain is what we are in most of the time, and I think that the bigger the pain, the more God you look for.

When you do something beautiful and nobody noticed, do not be sad. For the sun, every morning is a beautiful spectacle and yet most of the audience still sleeps.

Being honest may not get you a lot of friends but it'll always get you the right ones.

> I am a violent man who has learned not to be violent and regrets his violence.

My defenses were so great. The cocky rock and roll hero who knows all the answers was actually a terrified guy who didn't know how to cry. Simple.

The thing the '60s did was to show us the possibilities and the responsibility that we all had. It wasn't the answer. It just gave us a glimpse of the possibility.

It doesn't matter how long my hair is or what color my skin is or whether I'm a woman or a man.

I've withdrawn many times. Part of me is a monk, and part a performing flea! The fear in the music business is that you don't exist if you're not at Xenon with Andy Warhol.

"The reason why kids are crazy is because nobody can face the responsibility of bringing them up.

" I couldn't think of the next few years; it's abysmal thinking of how many years there are to go, millions of them. I just play it by the week. "

It looks like I'm going to be 40 and life begins at 40—so they promise. And I believe it, too.

> How can I go forward when I don't know which way I'm facing?

"I wouldn't say I was a born writer; I'm a born thinker.

Surrealism had a great effect on me because then I realized that the imagery in my mind wasn't insanity. Surrealism to me is reality.

"Time wounds all heels."

The trouble with government as it is, is that it doesn't represent the people. It controls them.

" Before Elvis there was nothing. "

> I believe in everything until it's disproved. So I believe in fairies, the myths, dragons. It all exists, even if it's in your mind. Who's to say that dreams and nightmares aren't as real as the here and now?

"If you want peace, you won't get it with violence.

" [On 'Help':] I meant it, it's real; the lyric is as good now as it was then. It's no different. And it makes me feel secure to know that I was that sensible, or whatever—not sensible, aware of myself. . . . It was just me singing 'Help' and I meant it. "

Everybody loves you when you're six foot in the ground.

" I don't want to grow up but I'm sick of not growing up . . . I'll find a different way of not growing up. "

You're just left with yourself
all the time, whatever you
do anyway. You've got
to get down to your own
God in your own temple.
It's all down to you, mate.

"I'm not really a career person; I'm a gardener, basically.

People are afraid of Beatle music. They are still afraid of my songs. Because they got that big image thing: You can't do a Beatle number . . . You can't touch a Lennon song; only Lennon can do it . . . It's garbage! Anybody can do anything.

Evolution and all hopes for a better world rest in the fearlessness and open-hearted vision of people who embrace life.

It matters not who you love, where you love, why you love, when you love or how you love, it matters only that you love.

"

As in a love affair, two creative people can destroy themselves trying to recapture that youthful spirit, at twenty-one or twenty-four, of creating without even being aware of how it's happening.

"

"Love is a promise, love is a souvenir, once given never forgotten, never let it disappear."

"Declare it. Just the same way we declare war. That is how we will have peace . . . we just need to declare it.

"

"If I can't have a fight with my best friend, I don't know who I can have a fight with.

"

"Well, I don't want to be king, I want to be real.

"I've always been a freak. So I've been a freak all my life and I have to live with that, you know. I'm one of those people.

"
My role in society, or any artist's or poet's role, is to try and express what we all feel. Not to tell people how to feel. Not as a preacher, not as a leader, but as a reflection of us all.

"

The more real you get, the more unreal the world gets.

> Get out there and get peace, think peace, and live peace and breathe peace, and you'll get it as soon as you like.

> I thought of nothing else but rock 'n' roll; apart from sex and food and money—but that's all the same thing, really.

A dream you dream alone is only a dream. A dream you dream together is reality.

"When I cannot sing my heart, I can only speak my mind.

"Nobody controls me. I'm uncontrollable. The only one who controls me is me, and that's just barely possible.

> You have to be a bastard to make it, and that's a fact.

Creativity is a gift. It doesn't come through if the air is cluttered.

I'm not afraid of death because I don't believe in it. It's just getting out of one car, and into another.

" Peace is not something you wish for; it's something you make, something you do, something you are, and something you give away.

"Tell the truth and make it rhyme."

 As usual, there's a great woman behind every idiot.

Our society is run by insane
people for insane objectives.
I think we're being run by
maniacs for maniacal ends and
I think I'm liable to be put away
as insane for expressing that.
That's what's insane about it.

> "Only by trying on other people's clothes do we find what size we are."

Nothing affected me until I heard Elvis. Without Elvis there would be no Beatles.

"There are two basic motivating forces: fear and love. When we are afraid, we pull back from life.

I don't believe in killing whatever the reason.

> The people have the power. All we have to do is awaken the power in the people.

Happiness is just how you feel when you don't feel miserable.

"Everyone deserves to believe they are beautiful."

We live in a world where we have to hide to make love, while violence is practiced in broad daylight.

"You can't give a child too much love and if you love somebody, you can't be with them enough. There's no such thing."

God is a concept by which we measure our pain.

> The main hangup in the world today is hypocrisy and insecurity.

I don't believe in yesterday, by the way.

If people take any notice of what we say, we say we've been through the drug scene, man, and there's nothing like being straight.

"Rituals are important. Nowadays it's hip not to be married. I'm not interested in being hip.

"There's nothing new under the sun. All the roads lead to Rome. And people cannot provide it for you. I can't wake you up. You can wake you up. I can't cure you. You can cure you."

Time you enjoy wasting is not wasted.

Everything they told me
as a kid has already been
disproved by the same
type of experts
who made them up in
the first place.

The pressures of being a parent are equal to any pressure on earth. To be a conscious parent, and really look to that little being's mental and physical health, is a responsibility which most of us, including me, avoid most of the time because it's too hard.

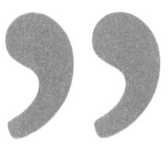

"There's an alternative to violence. It's to stay in bed and grow your hair.

"You can't just keep quiet about anything that's going on in the world unless you're a monk. Sorry, monks!"

"
It's fear of the unknown. The unknown is what it is. And to be frightened of it is what sends everybody scurrying around chasing dreams, illusions, wars, peace, love, hate, all that—it's all illusion. Accept that it's unknown and it's plain sailing.

"

"You won't get anything unless you have the vision to imagine it.

If everyone could just be happy with themselves and the choices people around them make, the world would instantly be a better place.

> Art is only a way of expressing pain.

Everything will be okay in the end. If it's not okay, it's not the end.

It's better to
fade away like
an old soldier
than to burn out.

If someone thinks that peace and love are just a cliché that must have been left behind in the '60s, that's a problem. Peace and love are eternal.

"War is over . . . if you want it.

" It's weird not to be weird. "

There are
no problems,
only
solutions.

"Yeah, we all shine on. Like the moon and the stars and the sun."

John Lennon

ABOUT THE EDITOR

Jade Riley is a writer whose interests include old movies, art history, vintage fashion and books, books, books.

Her dream is to move to London, to write like Virginia Woolf, and to meet a man like Mr. Darcy, who owns a vacation home in Greece.

www.ingramcontent.com/pod-product-compliance
Lightning Source LLC
Chambersburg PA
CBHW021131130526
44590CB00055B/359